POLY ME

The 48 Laws of Yummy & Relationships & A Guide to Real Love

LeShaun D. Pujoe'

Poly Me: The 48 Laws of Yummy and Relationships & A Guide to Real Love
© 2025 by **LeShaun D. Johnson**
All rights reserved.

No part of this publication may be reproduced, distributed, or transmitted in any form or by any means, including photocopying, recording, or other electronic or mechanical methods, without the prior written permission of the publisher, except in the case of brief quotations used in critical reviews and certain other noncommercial uses permitted by copyright law.

For permission requests, contact:
LeShaun D. Johnson

Published by LeShaun D. Johnson
Printed in the United States of America

ISBN: 979-8-218-73699-6

Cover Design: LeShaun D. Johnson
Author Photos: LeShaun D. Johnson
Interior Layout: LeShaun D. Johnson
Back Cover Design: LeShaun D. Johnson
First Edition: 2025

This is a work of nonfiction, inspired by personal experiences, perspectives, and reflections on relationships, intimacy, and the healing process. Any identifying details may have been changed to protect the privacy of individuals.

Dedicated…

To my Mama, who taught me that love isn't just a feeling, it's a hustle, a promise, and a legacy. Thank you for holding me down when the world tried to shake me up, for showing me what "ride or die" really means, and for reminding me every day that Yummy love started at home. I LOVE YOU and MISS YOU, Mama!

To my Uncle Link, whose laughter was louder than my doubts and whose wisdom slipped into my life like silk robes. Thank you for always believing in my shine and for teaching me how to play the game with heart and grind. Long live my Uncle, man.

To my Grandma Alma and Papa, whose love story wrote the first chapters of my own, thank you for modeling respect, resilience, and rhythm in relationships. Your devotion showed me that real love is a dance: sometimes slow, sometimes fast, but always in step with one another.

This book lives because of each of you. Your love for me, your significant others, and each other is my blueprint, your faith my fuel, and your stories my soundtrack. Wherever these pages go, your spirit rides shotgun. I love all of you forever.

Chapters

Intro: Welcome to a Yummy Type of Love 6
Law 1: The Foundation of the Game 8
Law 2: Understanding a Healthy Relationship? 10
Law 3: Define the Relationship You Crave. Clarity Is the First Seduction 11
Law 4: Know Your Attachment Style, Your Nervous System Has a Love Language 13
Law 5: Speak Yo' Love Language And Learn Theirs Too 18
Law 6: Don't Just Fall. Build That Sh*t from the Ground Up 21
Law 7: Dating in Modern Times 24
Law 8: Red Flags vs Green Flags: Check Ya Flag 26
Law 9: Toxicity vs Narcissism 28
Law 10: Chemistry vs Compatibility 30
Law 11: Building Trust Early 32
Law 12: Setting Boundaries from the Start 34
Law 13: Maintaining a Relationship 35
Law 14: The Goal is to Never Argue 37
Law 15: Nobody Wants an Argumentative Mouth 39
Law 16: Communication Styles and Active Listening 41
Law 17: Express and Listen 43
Law 18: Conflict Resolution Strategies and Solutions 45
Law 19: Emotional Labor and Balance 47
Law 20: Sexual Compatibility and Intimacy 49
Law 21: Dealing with Jealousy or Insecurity 52
Law 22: Nurturing Long-Term Commitment 54
Law 23: The Role of Humor and Playfulness 56
Law 24: Growth and Challenges 58
Law 25: Effort 60
Law 26: Personal Growth Within the Relationship 63
Law 27: Vulnerability is Sexy 65
Law 28: Relationships Are a Business (Navigating Finances Together) 67

Law 29: Cultural and Religious Differences 69
Law 30: Dealing with Trauma or Mental Health Issues 71
Law 31: Rebuilding After Trust is Broken 73
Law 32: Endings and New Beginnings 75
Law 33: When to Walk Away 77
Law 34: How to Break Up with Compassion 81
Law 35: Grieving a Lost Relationship 83
Law 36: Reclaiming Your Peace & Power 85
Law 37: Rebuilding Yourself After a Breakup 87
Law 38: Dating Yourself First 90
Law 39: Attracting Healthy Love Only 92
Law 40: Co-Parenting or Shared Responsibilities Post-Breakup 94
Law 41: Let Them Love You Loudly 96
Law 42: When Love Feels Safe 98
Law 43: Knowing When You're Ready Again 100
Law 44: The Art of Intentional Dating 102
Law 45: Stop Ignoring Your Intuition (The Gut Never Lies) 104
Law 46: Polyamory, Open Relationships & Ethical Non-Monogamy 106
Law 47: Keeping It Real About What You Want 109
Law 48: Gender Roles and Evolving Dynamics 111
Yummy's Type of Love is a Lifestyle, Not a Phase 114
Reflection and Rejection: The Yummy that Never Got Picked 116
Why I Wrote This Book: Inspired by Power, Game & Real Love 118
Acknowledgements 120
References 121

Welcome to a Yummy Type of Love

In a society influenced and driven by social media, relationships are evolving faster than most people's emotional intelligence. We swipe, we ghost, we chase, we settle, sometimes all in the same week. We talk about love, loyalty, and connection, but rarely do we sit down and dissect the rules we're playing by… or the ones we've inherited without question.

Poly Me: The 48 Laws of Yummy and Relationships is not your typical grandmother's love manual. It's for those who want to experience relationships, monogamous, polyamorous, or somewhere in the delicious in-between, with clarity, honesty, sensual awareness, and real power. It's about being "Yummy" with relationships: not just sexual, but self-aware, emotionally intelligent, and irresistibly grounded.

This book is built on Yummy's 48 core principles, laws, if you will, that will challenge how you see love, how you show up for others, and most importantly, how you show up for yourself. We'll explore the do's, the don'ts, and the "hell no's." We'll arm you with rebuttals to relationship myths that have kept people stuck, small, or silently suffering.

Whether you're poly-curious, deeply committed, freshly heartbroken, or just sick of dating like it's a bad job interview, this is your place. There's no judgment here, just hard truths, deep insights, and maybe a little sass.

You ready? Good. Let's get it, the Yummy way.

Law 1: The Foundation of the Game

"You can't build a solid foundation using Legos."
-Yummy

      Growing up we learned early on in school that every structure needs a good, solid foundation. Be it The Sears Tower, a family, or a throuple, all these things starts with a foundation. Without one, everything looks fine until life starts shaking it. And trust me, life gone shake it. I'm talking earthquake shake like the jokes people have bout me being big.

      The first law is simple, but not always easy: get grounded in who you are and what you want before you invite anyone else into your emotional architecture. Most people skip that part. They jump into love to escape loneliness, to feel seen, or because someone cute winked at them across a bar. That's human. But without inner clarity, connection becomes chaos. You can't win in love, or in life, if you ain't solid with you first. The realest game you'll ever run is the one you run on your own reflection. Too many folks jumping in relationships looking for somebody to complete them, when they ain't even complete on their own.

Ask yourself:

What do I really want from a relationship like honestly?

What am I ready to give or give up?

What are the non-negotiables for me?

Am I still carrying old wounds, trauma, or baggage that I haven't even acknowledged or tried to heal?

Foundations aren't glamorous. They're not the fly first date or the "we stayed up all night caking" type shit. But they are the difference between a relationship that survives pressure and one that crumbles the moment desire fades or conflict appears.

If you're exploring polyamory, this matters even more. Clear communication, emotional regulation, and radical honesty aren't optional; they're survival tools. Without a solid foundation, poly can turn into a messy escape from accountability instead of an expansive journey of intimacy.

The work starts with you. Before you set the tone for love, figure out who you are when no one else is around. That's your foundation. Don't chase love. Attract it by standing ten toes down in your truth. Start with self. Stay with self. That's how the game begins and that's how you win.

Law 2: Understanding a Healthy Relationship?

A healthy relationship, whether monogamous, polyamorous, or anything in between, isn't built on perfection; it's built on presence. It's the energy between two or more people who choose to show up for each other consistently, honestly, and without trying to control the outcome. A healthy relationship allows you to breathe. You don't shrink in it, you stretch, you grow, and you glow.

In this chapter of a "Yummy" style love life, the real flex is knowing that mutual respect is sexier than control. You know it's healthy when you feel emotionally safe to say what's on your mind without walking on pins and needles. When your "no" is just as respected as your "yes." When your joy isn't dimmed, but celebrated.

In poly dynamics, especially, healthy means clear communication, secure boundaries, and the freedom to be your full self, not half of someone else's fantasy. Jealousy might pop up, but it's acknowledged, not weaponized. Time, love, and energy are shared with care, not secrecy or guilt.

A healthy relationship is a partnership, not a power struggle. It's accountability without shame, affection without condition, and honesty without cruelty. It supports your peace, aligns with your values, and honors your identity.

Whether you're dating one person or dancing with a constellation of connections, the foundation must feel solid. If it doesn't, it's not love, it's a lesson.

Law 3: Define the Relationship You Crave. Clarity Is the First Seduction

Before you dive into a relationship or several, know what you're easing into. A lot of heartbreak, confusion, and late-night texting marathons come from skipping this essential step: identifying the type of relationship you truly desire. Not what you've been told to want. Not what you think is trendy or safe. What you, in your most desired, juicy, complex glory, want.

Ask yourself:

Do I crave emotional intimacy, sexual connection, or both?

Am I looking for one deep anchor relationship, or a collection of connections?

Do I need structure and titles, or do I thrive in fluidity?

Am I solo, poly, a relationship rebel, hierarchical, monogamish, or something totally new?

Naming what you want doesn't mean locking yourself into a box; it means you're drawing your own map. Relationships without intention drift into disappointment. With intention, they flourish.

Take this law seriously: desire without direction leads to entanglement, not intimacy. Whether you're seeking a dominant partner, a nesting companion, a kinky situationship, or a rotating roster of sexual joys, own it.

Your "Yum" may not look like anyone else's. That's the point. Be honest. Be specific. Be brave. Once you know what you want, you'll recognize who can meet you there and who can't.

Decide it, define it, and then dive in it.

Law 4: Know Your Attachment Style, Your Nervous System Has a Love Language

"My problem is I get too attached." – Yummy

You can't build pleasing, nourishing relationships if you don't understand the way you attach. Your attachment style is like your emotional GPS, it tells you how you respond to closeness, distance, and perceived threats in intimacy. And in polyamorous or non-traditional dynamics, where emotions get layered, this awareness becomes crucial. When it comes to love, your style is loud and clear.

Let's keep it all the way real. The way you act in relationships ain't random; it's your attachment style, bookie. That's your emotional blueprint, the way your heart and head deal with love, space, and stress. And listen, everybody got a type. There are four known attachment styles. Which one are you?

Secure: You chillin'. You trust people, talk it out, and don't lose your mind when ya lil yeah don't text back in 5 seconds. You can love deep and let folks breathe. This is the "I'm good either way" vibe. Unbothered, moisturized, in their lane.

Anxious: You love hard... maybe too hard. As soon as bae gets a little quiet, you already spiraling like, "Are they ghosting me??" You texting, rereading convos, and stalking their social media. You're not crazy, you just hate feeling abandoned. (We see you, baby.)

Avoidant: You the "ion need nobody" type...the "too hard for emotions" kind.. until somebody gets close, then you ghostin'. You cool with hookups, but when emotions pop off, you start feeling trapped. Deep down, you care, but showing it? Whew Chile, that's your struggle.

Fearful-Avoidant (aka Disorganized and unassure): Whew, mayne. You want love but don't trust it. One minute you all in, next minute you panicking and pushing people away. It's giving "come here, now get out." You're passionate, but lowkey paranoid love gonna hurt you. You tired and you know it.

No style is "bad," but each comes with patterns you must recognize if you want to grow beyond them. Polyamory doesn't "fix" attachment wounds, it reveals them. Fast. If you feel triggered when your partner goes on a date, doesn't text back quickly, or connects deeply with someone else, that's your nervous system sending you information. Instead of shaming yourself or blaming your partner, get curious.

This law isn't about fixing yourself. It's about knowing yourself, so you can communicate your needs, set boundaries with love, and show up for others without abandoning yourself.

Awareness is the first act of emotional responsibility. Know your pattern. Then choose your response.

So What's Your Love Style, Frfr?

Answer these like you texting your bestie. No filters, just vibes. Be honest your future bae (or baes) will thank you.

1. When somebody I like starts acting real close, I usually…

a) Cool, cool, I'm vibin'.

b) Oop! Now I'm thinking, "They gon' leave me."

c) Backs up slowly. This too much.

d) OMG yes wait, nah, OMG no, ugh, IDK.

2. When my person says they need space, I…

a) Respect it and go do me.

b) Text them 27 times and then cry.

c) Say "bet" and disappear for 3 days.

d) Panic, then block them, then unblock them, then panic again.

3. I feel the safest in relationships when…

a) We communicate and trust is solid.

b) They're all up on me, every day, no gaps.

c) I got freedom and control, period.

d) Things are spicy, dramatic, and a lil messy (lowkey).

4. My biggest fear in love is…

a) Losing that healthy connection.

b) Being left or forgotten.

c) Getting trapped or losing my freedom.

d) Opening up and getting my heart snatched (again).

Your Love Vibe:

Mostly A's: You that girl/guy/them with a Secure style. Grown and grounded.

Mostly B's: You got that Anxious sauce. Loyal AF but scared of being left on read—emotionally and literally.

Mostly C's: Big Avoidant energy. You love... from afar.

Mostly D's: Whew. You got that Fearful-Avoidant flavor, your heart's a Libra, Scorpio or Sagiterrorist. Sweet, chaotic, and complicated.

Now Let's Get Into Your Business (Journaling Time):

Pull out that notebook or open your Notes app and answer these:

When I catch feelings, what's my go-to drama? (Do I chase? Run? Ghost? Obsess?)

What situations make me feel unsafe or insecure in love?

What would it look like to feel safe and seen in a relationship?

What's one pattern I wanna break… and what would I do instead next time?

Law 5: Speak Yo' Love Language And Learn Theirs Too

"What we do for each other before marriage is no indication of what we will do after marriage." – Gary Chapman

Listen up, baby girl, love don't always sound like "I love you." Sometimes it's "Did ya eat today?" or "I organized everything the way you like it." That's the thing about them love languages they ain't always loud, but they damn sure matter.

The Love Man Gary Chapman gave us the OG Five Love Languages, but we finna remix em, put a little "Yum" to it, some vibes, playa life we livin'. You gotta know the things I like. That is what knowing love languages is all about. If your people ain't feeding you the way you receive love, you gon' stay starving, even in a full relationship.

Here's the rundown:

The 5 Love Languages (Yummy's Perspective)

1. Words of Affirmation:

Bae, go head tell me I'm fine. Make my head big. Tell me I'm handsome and you want me. If you say the right things, I'm floating on cloud 9. Compliments, encouragement, and surprise video attachments? Man, I'm yours forever.(Possibly, Lol)

2. Acts of Service:

Don't just say it. Show them. Fix my plate, bring me food, send that "I got you" Zelle when I'm down on my ass. It's the little things like Ella Mai say. Prove your love with effort, not shared social media posts saying you do these things and don't.

3. Receiving Gifts:

It ain't about the price, it's about the thought, the effort. Pull up with my favorite food? I'm yours. Surprise me with some shoes? Say less. It's giving "I saw this and thought of you." Girl gone pull these boxers to the side.

4. Quality Time:

I don't care if we chillin' on the couch or running errands, just be with me. No phones. No half-listening. Just vibe with me, fully. Time is currency, and I'm expensive.

5. Physical Touch:

Hold my hand, be clingy, be all up under me while I'm writing this book. I need that skin-to-skin. If you ain't tryna touch, don't even try to talk. Period.

Know Yours. Know Theirs.

The biggest problem in relationships? Folks be lovin' people in the way they like, not how their bae actually receives love. You might be dropping bands, and they just want a hug. You texting love notes, and they waiting for a damn cuddle.

In poly or open setups, you gotta learn multiple languages, like a whole love Rosetta Stone. Every partner may speak different emotional dialects, and if you don't learn them, miscommunication gon' ruin your lil poly paradise fast.

Real Talk Reflection: What's YOUR Love Language?

Take 10 mins and ask yourself:

What makes me feel the most loved when someone says it, does it, buys it, spends time, or touches me?

What do I give others when I'm in love? Is it the same or different from what I need?

Have I told my partners how I receive love, or am I just hoping they guess right?

Bottom Line:

You better learn how you like to be loved, then teach it. Don't suffer in silence when your love tank on E. Communicate. Translate. Elevate.

Closed mouths don't get fed and closed hearts don't get loved right.

Law 6: Don't Just Fall. Build That Sh*t from the Ground Up

Starting a new relationship? Whew, mayne. The butterflies be butterflying, the texts are giving serotonin, and you're already naming your future babies in your head. It's cute and all that… but whoa pump your brakes playa. Real connections don't come from fantasies. It comes from intention.

See falling in love is easy. Building love? That's grown-folks work there. When you begin a new relationship especially in a poly, monogamous or nontraditional setup, you gotta set the tone early. Otherwise, you'll end up deep in a situationship you never signed up for, asking the group chat, "Am I trippin', or…?" Let me set some ground rules for ya when kicking this thing off wit ya possible forever person.

Relationship Ground Rules (Day One Energy):

1. Be Real from the Start:

Don't be out here showing up as a doppelganger. Show up as you. Messy hair, emotional scars, weird kinks or whatever it is you carry. You don't need to be perfect, just honest.

2. Define the Vibe:

Y'all feeling each other, cool, but what is it tho? Is this a situationship? A play partner? Ya main? Shacking? Don't assume, ask. We not just going with the flow anymore. Especially if we don't even know where the river is leading.

3. Talk Structure Early:

Monogamish? Hierarchical? Exclusive? Open? Solo poly with a sprinkle of chaos? Spell. It. Out. Whatever it is. If you wait until you're six orgasms deep to talk about structure, you're already waaaayyyy behind.

4. Set Boundaries & Safe Words—Emotionally Too:

What are your "hell no's" and non-negotiables? What makes you spiral? What do you need when you're overwhelmed? Say it now, not mid-argument.

5. Stay Curious, Not Controlling:

New love is exciting, but don't try to own it. Ask questions. Learn their triggers, their dreams, their daily affirmations and reassurances. Choose connection over control. Every damn time.

Day One Questions You Should Be Asking:

What do you want right now in your life?

What does love look like for you?

What do your other relationships look like?

How do you handle conflict?

What does a "bad day" look like for you, and how can I support you through one?

Big Reminder:

      Don't lose yourself trying to become "the one" for someone (I'm speaking from personal experience). You are the one for you first. Build a connection where you can show up fully, be held in return, and grow without performing. Because we not doing starter-pack love any more. We're building luxury-level intimacy from day ONE.

Here's the Law:

Start it slow, build it real, and let the vibes speak facts, not fantasy.

Law 7: Dating in Modern Times

"It's giving... situationship with a side of delulu."
-Some random female on Facebook

Let's be honest here, modern dating ain't nothing like it use to be when we were growing up. Back in the day, you'd meet somebody at an event (cookouts, concerts, movies, etc.), they'd write their number on a napkin, and bam, you might have a whole family before the year's out. Now? You meet someone on a dating app, talk for three weeks, fall in love over shared posts, argue over a TikTok about dating, and ghost each other before the first link-up.

Let's talk the facts though.

Everybody's outside, but nobody wants to catch feelings. Folks are swiping like they're shopping on Shein, add to cart, remove, repeat. Texting is dry, communication is a struggle, and consistency? Baby girl, that's extinct. One day she texting, "grand rising king," the next day she "I fell asleep" at 6:37 PM. Like, ma'am, do you want love or just vibes, cash apps, and simp motion? Because this ain't that.

But don't get it twisted, we're not just victims of the game. We playing too.

Ladies, we got rosters like the Payne Gang. Fellas, y'all got five main girls and still complaining about loneliness. Everybody wanna be toxic 'cause it's trending, but deep down, we all just want someone to text us back without playing mind games.

Here's the law:

Modern dating is a jungle gym of red flags and ego trips. You gotta date like a playa but love like a legend. Be clear about what you want, stay 10 toes down on your standards, and don't let these emotionally unavailable folks trick you into thinking you asking for too much.

If it feels like a game, don't be afraid to be the coach. Call the plays, set the rules, and cut anybody that can't follow directions. 'Cause in this era, if you ain't careful, you'll end up catching feelings for someone who don't even know their own love language.

So stay playa, stay woke, and keep your heart where your standards live. And remember dating in 2025? It's survival of the Playa-est(Sadly).

Law 8: Red Flags vs Green Flags: Check Ya Flag

" Love is blind, it will take over your mind, what you think is love may truly not be, you need to elevate and find." -Eve and Faith Evans

Let's get into this one. 'Cause some of y'all(both men and women) be out here ignoring red flags like they some cute lil Valentine's Day flowers or something. Nah. That ain't romantic, that's delusional as hell. You saw the signs, you just wanted to play optometrist and pretend they ain't exist.

He don't text back for three days? "He probably just busy."
She got a whole man but swears they "basically broken up"? "We just vibin' for now."
NO. That's not a vibe, that's a walking, talking red flag parade with unicorn glitter on it.

Let me break it down in Yummy terms:

Red Flags:

- Inconsistent communication (only hit you up when convenient)
- Love bombing then ghosting (baby girl, this ain't Build-a-Bae)
- No accountability ("That's just how I am." OK, and?)
- Talking bad about all their exes (you gon' be next)
- Jealous, possessive, or always testing your loyalty like you the Praxis

If the energy is off, trust your gut. Don't confuse "passion" with chaos. That's not deep, it's draining.

Green Flags:

- Clear intentions (no mystery, no "let's see where it goes" every month)
- Consistency (calls when they say they will, shows up every time)
- Emotional maturity (can talk through problems without turning into WWIII)
- Supports your dreams, not just your body
- Listens with their whole chest, not just their ears

Green flags don't always come with fireworks. Sometimes it's just peace, safety, and feeling like your whole self around them. And if that feels boring to you? You might be addicted to dysfunction. Fix that. Ain't nothing Playa about that.

Here's the law:
If it doesn't serve your peace, it's a red flag in disguise.
Stop turning trauma into romance. Stop calling red flags "personality traits." And stop ignoring the people who actually treat you right, 'cause they don't bring drama with their affection.

Protect your energy like it's family jewels.
Not everybody deserves access just 'cause they know how to flirt and lie in 4K. Recognize the red, respect the green, and don't ever let confusion feel like chemistry. Remember, even if you squint ya eyes at those red flags long enough, they still gonna be red.

Law 9: Toxicity vs Narcissism

"Confusing demon with damaged is nasty work."
-Yummy

Let's stop confusing "healing" with hell. Everybody wanna throw around the word "narcissist" like it's the latest zodiac sign, but mannnn listen, there's levels to this bullshit. Not every toxic person is a narcissist, but every narcissist is absolutely toxic and dangerous if you don't know how to clock it.

Toxic? That's someone with bad habits, unhealed wounds, and probably no business dating right now. Narcissist? That's someone who will emotionally drain your soul, gaslight you into questioning your reality, and still have the audacity to act like YOU did something to them.

Let me break it down like a hood YUM Talk:

Toxic People Be Like:

- Mad jealous over your grow-up/glow-up
- Apologize, but keep doing the same shit
- Play victim when you call them out
- Use your love as leverage (manipulation 101)
- Say "I'm working on myself" while ruining your peace

Toxicity is like secondhand smoke. You ain't gotta light it to catch the effects. But sometimes they can change if they do the work (most don't, but hey).

Narcissists Be Like:

- Never wrong. Ever. (Even when caught in 4K)
- Love bomb you, then discard you like takeout
- Gaslight game strong ("You're too sensitive." "That never happened.")
- Need constant praise, but give nothing back
- Got a whole double life and still think they the victim

Mess around with a narcissist and you'll lose your mind thinking you the problem. You'll be journaling, praying, Googling the wildest things, meanwhile they're sleeping peacefully, unbothered, unfazed, and probably cheating.

Here's the law:
Stop making excuses for people who bring chaos and call it "love." If you always feel confused, depleted, or like you walking on eggshells, it ain't growth, it's war. And love ain't supposed to feel like survival.

Toxicity is a storm. Narcissism is a setup.
Protect your peace like God said it's your last day here on earth. Some people don't need closure, they need consequences. And the best revenge? Growing up and going ghost.

Your sanity is not up for negotiation. Period.

Some folks ain't meant to be healed, just deleted. Block 'em physically, spiritually, and digitally.

Law 10: Chemistry vs Compatibility

"Don't get it twisted, them vibes be lying too."- Yummy

Let's keep it real, just 'cause y'all got hella chemistry, don't mean y'all supposed to be anything more than a memory. That spark? That late-night convo with the soft voice and the playlist hitting just right? That moment when your heart did the Tamia "When I think about you" 2 step, 'cause they looked at you a certain way? Yeah… that's chemistry. But that doesn't mean they got the tools to build a life, communicate during conflict, or even know how to love you past the honeymoon vibes.

Chemistry is cute. Compatibility is committed.

You can have chemistry with someone who ain't got no emotional intelligence, no job, and no intentions. You can vibe with a walking red flag easily. You can fall for someone who only fits your wounds, not your future.

That's why some of y'all be like:
"I don't know why I can't leave them alone..."
It's because your trauma is attracted to their chaos, and y'all got chemistry in dysfunction. That ain't love, that's a karmic connection with a good beat.

Now compatibility? That's when your values align, your lifestyles work together, and your peace is protected. Even when the passion ain't on 100 every day. It's slow-burning, solid, and sometimes boring to the unhealed eye. But it's the kind of boring that builds empires, not situationships.

Here's the law:
If they excite you but can't stabilize you, that's not your person. It's your lesson.
Start checking for character, not just chemistry.
'Cause the real flex? Being turned on by peace, patience, and someone who follows through. Don't let them butterflies and that cloud nine ideology distract from the fact that y'all don't even want the same life.

Law 11: Building Trust Early

Let's talk about trust, because some of y'all out here handing out access like club flyers, then crying when folks fumble you like a wet football.

Look playa, trust ain't something you give just 'cause they fine, consistent for two weeks, or got a smooth voice. That's not trust. That's hope with a lace front, it looks good, but boy, it ain't secured yet.

Building trust early doesn't mean moving fast; it means moving smart.

Ask the real questions. Watch how they move when you say "no." Pay attention to what they do when you're not around, not just what they say when they wanna smash. Trust is built in the quiet moments: the callbacks, the consistency, the corrections without ego, the honesty when it's inconvenient.

And let's be clear:

You don't gotta "test" people with fake drama or setups to see if they loyal. Y'all got that bad. That's insecurity, not intuition. You build trust by being trustworthy yourself, not by playing emotional FBI.

Trust early, but verify. Open the door, but don't throw away your security system. Let them earn the deeper parts of you. Don't trauma-bond. Don't overshare just to feel close. Don't mistake a trauma story for a trust badge.

Here's the law:
Early trust should feel earned, not rushed. If they're real, they won't rush your walls, they'll respect your gate.

Law 12: Setting Boundaries from the Start

Let's clear something up real quick: boundaries are not being mean.
They're not walls, they're filters. You can be sweet and have standards. You can be loving and still say, "Nah, I don't play like that."

When you don't set boundaries early, you are teaching people how to play with you. They'll think "She's cool with that" or "He doesn't mind" when you just ain't wanna come off pressed. Newsflash: closed mouths get disrespected.

Here's what boundaries from the jump look like:

- Saying what you're not okay with before it happens again.
- Not rearranging your whole life for a maybe.
- Letting "no" be a complete sentence, not a negotiation.
- Not letting vibes override your values.

And listen, if they get mad at your boundaries? They were planning to benefit from your lack of them. That ain't your person, that's a red flag in a wife-beater or a sundress.

You gotta teach people how to treat you from the gate. Not after they mess up. Not after you're already hurt. Do it when you're still smiling, so they know your peace ain't up for debate.

Here's the law:
Set the tone early, or they'll set it for you.
Boundaries don't push real ones away; they weed the weak ones out.

Law 13: Maintaining a Relationship

"Consistent love is peaceful love. Passion can fade. Maintaining consistency will keep the flame lit." – Yummy

Now we getting into the nitty gritty of this thang. Everybody wanna fall in love, but don't nobody hardly ever talk about staying in love.

Let's be honest, starting a relationship is easy as hell for the most part. It starts off giving butterflies, date nights, matching hoodies, inside jokes, playlists, etc. Easy right? But maintaining a relationship? That's crazy work. That's choosing each other when the vibe is off. That's showing up when it's not all fun and games or sexy. That's accountability and affection.

People out here breaking up over little arguments, ghosting over miscommunication, or silently resenting their partner instead of just talking it out. Like, damn girl was it love, or was it just good aesthetics?

Here's the real tea(clock it):

Maintenance means checking the emotional oil and communicating before it explodes. Re-learning your person as they grow. Giving grace. Scheduling quality time like it's a job. Doing the boring stuff that builds the beautiful stuff.

You maintain your hair. Your car. Your nails. Your vibe. So why you think your relationship gon' thrive on like a Tesla on autopilot?

And peep this, a maintained relationship brings peace. Real peace. Not fake "we ain't arguing" silence, but that "I got you, you got me" calm. That "we're good even when life ain't" energy.

When you put in the work, love stops being chaotic and starts being grounding.

Here's the law:

Love is like your favorite car or slab that you treat with love and care daily. If you don't maintain it, don't be surprised when it breaks down.

Law 14: The Goal is to Never Argue

"Clapbacks Don't Build Connection"- Yummy

Let's clear this up real quick: "Never argue" don't mean you'll never disagree. It means you don't let disagreement turn into emotional street fights, screaming contests, or silent treatment sagas.

We grown now. We ain't gotta raise voices to raise awareness. Arguing is a loud ego. Communication is quiet power. The goal is to understand, not to win. This ain't a versuz or rap battle. You not battling your person. You supposed to be on the same damn team. Why you treating bae like an opp?

When you argue constantly, you don't build love, you build resentment. That "I didn't mean it" after all that yelling and belittling don't hit the same when it's the third time this week. Words leave bruises you can't see. Tone leaves tension in the room long after the convo ends.

Mature love? That's:

"Let's pause, I need a minute."

"I hear you, even if I don't agree."

"I'm not attacking, I'm explaining."

"Let's solve the problem, not destroy each other."

It ain't weak to walk away from a fight. It's powerful to protect the connection even while processing conflict. That's grown, sexy, and peaceful.

Here's the law:

If you gotta argue to feel heard, it's already off. Talk soft. Listen deep. Protect the bond while solving the issue. Disagree without disrespect. If it's gone cost you your peace, it ain't worth proving.

Law 15: Nobody Wants an Argumentative Mouth

"Mouth too loud, love too weak." -Yummy

Let's stop acting like being loud, combative, disrespectful, and always "keeping it real" is a personality trait. It's not. It's a defense mechanism wrapped in trauma and attitude.

Nobody wants to feel like they're in a verbal boxing match every time they talk to you. Relationships ain't debates. Your partner ain't your punching bag. And no, "I'm just passionate" is not a valid excuse for acting like a whole bully.

Constant backtalk, slick comebacks, disrespectful name-calling, and trying to have the last word? That's not cute. That's exhausting. You could be the finest thing walking, but if your mouth is always looking for a fight, your presence becomes a problem.

Here's what a peaceful mouth looks like:

Knowing when to speak and when to chill.

Giving feedback, not flames.

Checking tone, not just facts.

Listening to understand, not just to reload.

And trust, real ones don't argue, they articulate. The grown and healed ain't finna stay where the energy always feels hostile, defensive, or emotionally unsafe.

Here's the law:

A loving mouth brings softness, not smoke. If every convo turns into conflict, you're not building love, you're building walls. Say girl, you're pretty asf, but it doesn't hit the same when your mouth is reckless and disrespectful. Peace is the new fine. But fellas, we're not innocent either. Calling your girl a b***h, hoe, or some disrespectful clown sh*t like that every time she tries to communicate her feelings with you ain't the move either. Ladies and gentlemen, if you start spewing disrespect or attacking the insecurities of your significant other when they are trying to communicate their feelings, you meant what you said when you said it. *Shrugs*

Law 16: Communication Styles and Active Listening

Remember when ole girl told Lebron to, "shut up and dribble"? Although I'll never agree with her on that at all, matter of fact, f*** her if we're being honest. That concept can apply for communication in relationships. More like, "Shut up and hear me out." Respectfully.

Man, some of y'all talk like it's a sport but listen like you on mute. Real talk, communication ain't just what you say, it's how you deliver it, and how you receive it. You could be spilling your whole heart, and if your tone off? Boom, defense mode. You could be hearing every word someone says, but if you ain't listening to understand, only to respond? That ain't communication, baby. That's a podcast with two hosts talkin' over each other.

Different people communicate differently:

Some folks need time to process.

Some need reassurance.

Some get quiet when they're hurt.

Some get loud 'cause they never felt heard.

The key to it all? Learning your person's language AND teaching them yours. That's real intimacy.

Active listening is a flex. It's when you:

Let them finish.

Ask real questions.

Reflect back what you heard.

Don't listen just to say, "That's not what I meant…"

It's hearing the pain behind the words, not just the volume.

And don't think communication is only what's said. Body language be screaming. Silence be loud. Reactions be writing books like this one I'm writing. Read the energy, not just the text thread.

Here's the law:

Communication styles matter. Listening is love. Talking is easy. Tuning in? That's grown behavior. Stop waiting for your turn to talk. Real love listens even when it's uncomfortable.

Law 17: Express and Listen

"Say It with Your Chest, Hear It with Your Soul"- Yummy

Let's stop playing tug-of-war with feelings, mmkay?

Healthy love ain't just about getting your point across. It's about creating space for both voices to matter. Expression and listening go hand in hand, like edges and gel. One without the other? Baby, it's messy.

Some of y'all wanna vent, pop off, cry, monologue, demand, and trauma dump, but when it's your turn to listen? You go ghost, defensive, or dry as hell. Nah, boo boo kitty. This ain't a solo act. This is a duet.

To express means:

Speak your truth, not your triggers.

Be clear, not cryptic.

Say what you need, not just what you hate.

Share your story without playing victim or villain.

To listen means:

Stop cutting folks off mid-sentence.

Don't twist their words to match your narrative.

Don't make it about you when it's not.

Actually hear what they're saying, not just what you fear they meant.

Real love is a safe space, not a stage.

You should feel free to speak and safe to be heard. That's how grown energy flows.

Here's the law:

Expression without listening is just noise. Listening without expression is suppression. Do both, or do neither. Say your piece, but stay present for theirs. That's where the healing lives.

Law 18: Fix It Without Fighting

"Let's Argue… Like Adults"- Yummy

Let's get the business clear. Conflict is inevitable. Drama is optional.

Y'all gon' bump heads. That's life. But how you handle it? That's what separates toxic from ten toes down. You don't gotta explode, ghost, or throw a subliminal every time something feels off. Real ones don't run from problems. They solve them.

Here's how grown folks do conflict resolution:

Pause before you pop off. That deep breath be saving relationships.

Own your part. Even if it's 10%, hold it. Accountability is sexy.

Use "I" statements, not accusations. "I feel unheard" hits different than "You don't ever listen!"

Listen like you love them. Not like you tryna win.

Find solutions, not someone to blame. If y'all both lose, the argument was pointless.

And listen, some things ain't worth the drama.

You're fighting about laundry, but it's really about not feeling appreciated. You mad they went out, but it's really about needing quality time. Say what it's really about. Address the root, not just the reaction.

Sometimes the answer ain't in a fight. It's in a hug, a real convo, a plan, or some damn space.

Don't let your pride ruin something that could've been solved with a soft tone and a listening ear.

Here's the law:

Conflict is a test, not a trap. Solve it with love, not ego. That's what keeps it healthy. Don't fight to be right. Fight to be understood and then fight for peace.

Law 19: I'm Not Ya Mama or Ya Mental Health Plan

Let's get one thing straight: Emotional labor is real, and it's draining AF.

If one person is always carrying the convo, calming the storms, solving the moods, and being the "understanding one"... baby, that ain't a relationship. That's a damn internship in unpaid therapy.

Love shouldn't feel like a full-time job where only one of y'all showed up to clock in. We all got baggage. We all got trauma. But don't hand someone your whole suitcase and walk off like it's their job to unpack it.

Emotional labor looks like:

Always being the one to de-escalate.

Overexplaining your worth.

Constantly regulating your partner's mood while yours gets ignored.

Being the "strong one" to keep the peace.

Nah. Emotional balance means reciprocity. I support you, you support me. I hold space for you, you do the same for me. We don't dump, we pour, refill, and rotate.

'Cause let's be clear, being emotionally available is not the same as being emotionally used. You are not a rehab for broken people who don't wanna do the work.

Here's the law:

Emotional labor ain't love. Balance is. Match my energy, match my effort, and most importantly, match my healing. I'm not too much, you're just not doing enough. Meet me where the emotional effort is equal.

Law 20: Sexual Compatibility and Intimacy

Okay let's keep it a buck: Sex ain't everything... but it damn sure ain't nothing. I ain't gone lie I'm a very sexual person. It's not really a dealbreaker for me BUT I would love a woman that is sexually compatible enough with me that she can feed my sex drive. I definitely will feed hers.

Anyways, moving on, you can have deep convos, shared goals, aligned horoscopes, and still be out here like, "Umm... so when does the spark kick in?"

Sexual compatibility matters. Not just "are y'all smashing?", but is the connection real, the chemistry mutual, and the satisfaction shared? 'Cause listen, if one person's showing up with passion and the other with a top-tier playlist and no rhythm... man, somebody's gon end up sexually starved and spiritually salty.

Let's break it down:

Compatibility means you actually enjoy what y'all are doing together. It's about style, pace, frequency, preferences, AND comfort.

Intimacy means it's deeper than the stroke game. It's emotional, mental, spiritual, all of that. Can y'all touch each other's body and soul?

And don't get it twisted: you can have fire sex and still feel empty if there's no intimacy. And you can have intimacy, but if the sex life got less rhythm than a middle school dance? Holuppppp.

So talk about it:

What turns you on?

What shuts you down?

What do you need to feel safe, freaky, and fulfilled?

Closed mouths don't get kissed (or climaxed).

Here's the law:

Sexual energy and emotional intimacy must be in sync. Otherwise, y'all just roommates with benefits or worse, regrets. Don't just have sex, have connection. And if we not vibin' in the sheets, we not vibin' period.

Yummy Exercise: Between the Sheets & Beyond

Instructions:

Sit down with your partner (or your journal or Notes App, if you're single or preparing for love) and answer the following questions with honesty, no shame, and all the grown-folk energy:

Part 1: Talk That Talk

Rate the following (1-5)

1 = Not at all / 5 = Absolutely

I feel safe expressing my desires with my partner.

We regularly communicate about our sexual needs.

Our physical chemistry is mutual and exciting.

I feel emotionally connected during sex.

My boundaries are respected in and out of the bedroom.

Now discuss (or journal):

What does satisfying sex look like for me?

When do I feel the most desired?

Are there unspoken fantasies or fears I haven't shared?

Is anything missing that I'm afraid to admit?

Part 2: The Intimacy Inventory

Choose 3 things from this list to explore more deeply with your partner:

Favorite non-sexual forms of intimacy

Turn-ons and turn-offs

Ways to initiate intimacy (without pressure)

Sensual vibes (music, scent, touch, words, etc.)

One thing I want to try, but haven't asked for yet

Something I wish we did more after sex

Challenge:

Have a "No Judgement Intimacy Night." Talk first, then touch if the vibe is right. The goal is connection, not performance.

Law 21: Dealing with Jealousy or Insecurity

"Check Yourself Before You Wreck What You Got"- Yummy

Let's get one thing straight: jealousy and insecurity are human, but letting them run the show? That's terrible and tragic. You can't be mad at folks for having a past, for getting attention, or for being the full-course meal you signed up to devour.

Jealousy be like, "Who's that in their comments?"

Insecurity be like, "I'm probably not enough."

And together? They got you spiraling, creating drama outta vibes you never even confirmed.

But here's the truth:

Jealousy is often a signal, not a sentence.

It's your inner child, your past heartbreak, your unhealed wounds whispering, "Protect me."

You don't kill the jealousy, you talk to it, understand it, and handle it before it handles you.

Here's how you handle the green-eyed gremlin:

Pause before you react. Are they being shady, or are you projecting?

Speak from your feelings, not accusations. "I feel insecure" hits differently than "Who tf is that?"

Do a self-check: Is this about them or something you haven't healed?

Boost your self-worth. Confidence ain't cocky, it's clarity on your value.

Ask for reassurance if you need it, but don't demand it like a job interview.

Jealousy ain't always bad, it shows you care. But how you handle it? That's what separates sabotage from self-awareness.

Here's the law:

Jealousy and insecurity will pop up, but it's your job not to let them punk you outta a good thing. I can feel a way and still act grown. Emotion is human, and maturity is power.

Law 22: Nurturing Long-Term Commitment

Understand this: anybody can be cute for a couple weeks. But can you still love him/her when they're tired, moody, irritable, or busy? Can you hold it down when it ain't date night, but dishwashing and debt talk?

Commitment ain't just the title, it's the maintenance.
You water a plant, or it dies. You maintain a car, or it breaks down. Same with relationships. Don't let the honeymoon phase trick you into thinking the work stops when it "feels right."

Here's what nurturing long-term love really looks like:

- Showing up consistently, even when life gets loud.
- Choosing them daily, not just when it's convenient or Instagram-cute.
- Having hard convos with soft hearts.
- Knowing their love language, not just their favorite position.
- Keeping the spark alive without forcing the flame.

And let's be real: boredom happens.
Ruts happen. Bills, routines, work stress, life gon' life. But if the foundation is real? You won't go looking for new vibes, you'll go harder for what you got.

Here's the law:
Don't just fall in love, stay there. Nurture the bond as if it were your peace, your power, your legacy. 'Cause it is. Loyalty ain't loud, it's daily. Show up, grow up, and pour in without pause.

Law 23: The Role of Humor and Playfulness

Yessssss, now we talkin' about the secret sauce to keep a relationship from feeling like a board meeting with feelings. Welcome to Law 23, where we unlock the power of humor, inside jokes, and not taking everything so damn serious all the time! Because if you know me, then you know I play all the damn time. I'm nonchalant a lot because everything not so damn serious to me.

Let's keep it a buck: If y'all don't laugh together, y'all ain't built to last.
Ain't nothing sexier than a partner who can make you crack up mid-argument, or turn a rough day into a comedy show without even trying. That's a bond, baby. That's medicine.

Humor is glue.
It's the release. The reset. The reminder that this ain't war, it's love. You can be mad and still giggle. You can be stressed and still flirt. You can roast each other and still be obsessed. That's grown.

Here's how you keep playfulness alive:

- Send dumb memes and posts that only y'all would laugh at.
- Make up inside jokes that don't make sense to anyone but you two.
- Tickle, flirt, dance badly, make up songs in the kitchen.
- Have roast battles but with love. ("Boy if you don't….)

And don't get it twisted, playfulness is not immaturity. It's actually emotional intelligence on

100. It means you can have fun without disrespect. You can keep it light without losing the depth. You can bring joy without dropping the ball on real talk.

Because sometimes, the way back to love ain't a long convo, it's just a shared laugh and a lil booty pop to their favorite song in the mirror.

Here's the law:
If you can't laugh together, you won't last together. Keep it light. Keep it silly. Keep it us. You can't build forever with someone who don't know how to play. Joy is foreplay, baby.

Law 24: Growth and Challenges

Now we in the deep end, baby, because love ain't always soft. Sometimes it's a mirror. Sometimes it's a storm. But when it's real, it grows you. Welcome to Law 24: Growth and Challenges, aka the law where you either elevate together or evaporate apart.

Let's get into it: every relationship gon' hit a bump. Or a wall. Or a whole-ass identity crisis. You'll both change, evolve, and grow, and that's not the problem. The problem is when y'all don't grow in alignment.

See, growth looks different on everybody:

- One person might go to therapy, while the other's still sweeping stuff under the rug.
- One might be chasing purpose, while the other's stuck on autopilot.
- One might be healing... while the other still flexin' their trauma.

And when life throws lemons? Whew. You would think you can make lemonade but that's when you find out if you got a solid significant other or just a plus-one. Can y'all hold each other down through depression, job loss, family drama, and spiritual shifts?

Real love says:
"We're in this together, even when it's uncomfortable."
"Let's keep checking in, not just on us, but on who we're becoming."
"I'll fight with you, not against you."

Here's the law:
Challenges gon' come, growth is guaranteed. But how y'all navigate it together? That's what makes it love, not just a link-up. So don't run from the tough stuff. Let it grow you, sharpen you, and connect you on a soul level. Every challenge is a chance to choose each other again. Real love ain't scared of the upgrade.

Law 25: Effort

"Love don't work unless you do." -Yummy

Yuuup! Know y'all was ready for this one. I bet the ladies is yelling "Yaaaaasssssss" lol. Let's talk about effort. The thing that separates a fling from a forever, a crush from a commitment, and a "wyd" text from actual intentions. Because Law 25 is all about putting in that real energy, not just lip service and vibes. As we dig deeper into effort, real ones know sustained energy is what keeps love juicy, not just the chase.

Let's be real, effort is sexy. Text them first. Plan the date. Remember what they said they liked. Show up when you say you will. Put some damn seasoning on this connection! We're done entertaining folks who think "low effort" is a personality type. No more dry convos, lazy energy, or folks who think presence = participation. Nah, that ain't it.

Effort is giving:

- "I thought of you, so I bought this."
- "Let me know you got home safe."
- "I know your love language and I speak it fluently."
- "I'm showing up for us, even when I'm tired, because you matter."

It don't gotta be grand. Just consistent. Intentional. Real.
Flowers are cute and all. But effort? Effort is taking the time to understand me. To show care when no

one's watching. To ask questions and actually listen. To bring us into the room. Not just yourself.

You wanna know if someone's serious? Watch their effort.
And you wanna keep something good? Match it. Elevate it. Pour into it.

Listen. Effort don't end after the first 90 days. That's not a probation period, it's just your opening audition. If you can't maintain the same energy that you used to get them, you definitely won't keep them.

Effort is not exhausting when it comes from the right place.
When it's real, it's not about perfection. It's about intention.
It's about:

- Remembering the small stuff.
- Holding space on their bad days.
- Caring about what matters to them, even when it doesn't directly benefit you.
- Asking, "What do you need today?" without assuming the answer is always sex, silence, or space.

And look, sometimes people really think they're doing enough. But intent without effort still equals neglect. You don't get points for "trying in your head." Show up where it counts.

Yum Tip: Effort is love in motion.
Not just words. Not just gestures. It's what you do when the mood's not cute, the vibes ain't vibing, and you still decide to try.

If you're always the one initiating, planning, fixing, or feeling? Baby, you're not in a relationship, you're in a performance. And that's not love. That's labor.

The ones who want you, show it.
The ones who value you, prove it.
The ones who see forever, work for it.

Here's the law:

Love requires motion. It ain't a vibe you sit in, it's an energy you invest. No effort? No access. Ain't nothing more attractive than someone who actually gives a damn out loud, on purpose, and every day. Effort is the difference between being wanted and being kept. And if you gotta beg for effort? That ain't your person, it's a project.

Law 26: Personal Growth Within the Relationship

"Grow with me or get left at the last version." – Yummy

This law is about healing, evolving, and leveling TF up without leaving your relationship behind. Because one of the biggest myths out here is that "finding love means you're done growing." Uh-uh. Nah. Nope. Real love makes room for your becoming. Being in love should never mean losing yourself.

Let's get one thing straight: you don't stop being YOU just because you're in a relationship. This ain't prison. This ain't a soul tie from 2005. This ain't "death row", this is "we rising, individually and together." Period.

Personal growth in a relationship means:

- You still get to chase your dreams.
- You still get to evolve your mindset.
- You still get to heal parts of you they didn't break.
- You still get to glow up mentally, emotionally, spiritually, and financially, without guilt.

Because what's the point of being in love if it don't water you, challenge you, and clap for you at the same damn time?

Now don't get it twisted, growth ain't always aesthetic. Sometimes it's ugly-crying in therapy. Sometimes it's realizing, "Damn, I used to shut down instead of speak up."

It's doing the inner work while still making space for connection.

And a real one? They gon' cheer for the new you, even if the old version was more convenient. They gon' hold space while you evolve, not compete with your healing. They gon' grow too, because y'all inspire each other to do better, not guilt-trip each other into staying the same.

Here's the law:

Your relationship should be a greenhouse, not a cage. If love doesn't let you grow, it's not love, it's a lid. If I gotta lose myself to love you, I'd rather love me louder.

Law 27: Changing Dynamics Over Time

Now we talking about grown and seasoned love, not just "day one" energy but that real deal, real-time, we're-changing-but-still-choosing-each-other kinda vibe. Law 27 is all about embracing the evolution of your connection as life shifts, moods change, and both of y'all level up, fall off, come back, re-learn, and rediscover each other again and again.

Let's be honest: how y'all start ain't how y'all gon' finish.
And that's not a bad thing. That's called evolution. Relationships don't stay the same because people don't stay the same.

Life be life-ing. People grow, priorities shift, babies happen, healing starts, bills stack, trauma pops back up, and new goals form. And through it all, your dynamic has to stretch, not snap.

What once was:

- Late-night convos turns into "We gotta talk before we crash out."
- Freaky Fridays turn into "Can we nap together in peace?"
- Texting all day turns into quality time in shorter, deeper bursts.
- The clingy lover might become more independent.
- The avoidant one might become more emotionally present.

And guess what?
That's beautiful AF if y'all allow the shifts.

The problem is that people fall in love with a version of someone, not realizing that love is a series of re-introductions. You gotta stay curious. Stay open. Keep choosing each other through every phase.

Here's the law:
You won't love the same way forever and that's the point. Change is not the enemy. Disconnection is. So check in. Recalibrate. Update the "us." Grow the bond to match the version of y'all that exists right now.

Law 28: Relationships Are a Business (Navigating Finances Together)

Love without a money convo is just vibes, and vibes don't pay rent. Welcome to Law 28: Relationships are a Business, where we talk coin, credit, and commitment because love gotta make sense and cents. Period.

Let's stop pretending like romance without financial harmony is just expensive confusion. You can't build a legacy on cute selfies and couple trips alone. If the money messy, the relationship gets stressful real fast.

Being boo'd up means being:

- Transparent about spending habits.
- Realistic about who pays what and why.
- Willing to grow that credit, save that coin, and invest in y'all's future.

Every relationship is part business, baby.
Not in a cold way, but in an innovative way.
Because bills gon' come. Emergencies hit. Life shifts. And if y'all can't talk money without catching an attitude? Y'all ain't ready for marriage. Y'all barely ready for the lease.

And this goes both ways:

- If your partner's winning, be a support, not a weight.
- If you're the breadwinner, don't weaponize that check.
- If y'all both broke, get creative, grind together, and be transparent.

It's not about who makes more. It's about who moves smart.
Split what makes sense. Share what's fair. And most importantly: have the damn money talk early. Before it turns into resentment, ego, or an eviction notice.

Here's the law:
Love is emotional, yes. But it's also logistical. So get on the same page financially, or get out of each other's pockets. And stop that damn "50/50" and "Man pay all the bills" bullshit. That particular conversation has always been stupid. *Shrugs*

Law 29: Respect Cultural and Religious Differences

Okay now we're talking love that crosses worlds, upbringings, languages, and spiritual paths, because when hearts connect across cultures and faiths, it can be beautiful... and also messy if y'all are not real about it. Welcome to Law 29, where we unpack respect, understanding, and the work it takes to blend lives, not just vibes.

Imagine you fell for someone outside your culture, your faith, or your background. Cute. Beautiful. Powerful. But also: you better come correct. Because love across lines means double the awareness and triple the respect.

You can't just be in love with the aesthetic of their culture, you need to respect the reality of it. That means:

- Learning their values, not just the food.
- Understanding their holidays, not just showing up for the outfits.
- Navigating spiritual practices with curiosity, not condescension.
- Respecting family dynamics, traditions, boundaries, even when they clash with yours.

The same goes for religion. If you're unequally yoked, spiritually speaking, you need to ask:

- Can we raise kids with harmony?
- Can we coexist without tension?
- Do I respect their faith even if I don't follow it?

Love can bridge differences, but it can't bulldoze them.
Don't enter someone's cultural or religious space thinking your way is "better" or more "normal." That's colonizer behavior.

When it works? Ooooh, it's magic. It's growth. It's legacy.
But it don't work without:
Conversations
Compromises
Curiosity over criticism

Here's the law:
You can love someone deeply and still clash culturally if you don't do the work. Admiration without understanding turns into conflict. So don't just date the person, learn their world. If you can't love my roots, don't touch my petals.

Law 30: Dealing with Trauma or Mental Health Issues

Love ain't always pretty. Sometimes it's about sitting in the hard, healing through the ugly, and staying when it's easier to run. Law 30 is not for the faint. This is for the real ones who know relationships can either be a healing space or a hurting place, depending on how you handle it.

Everybody's healing from something. Trauma ain't always visible, but it's always real. And mental health? That's not just a trending social media word. It's a real battle for a lot of people trying to love and be loved.

Let's make one thing clear:
Your partner is not your therapist.
And you are not theirs.

But you can be:

- A safe space
- A soft place to land
- Someone who respects boundaries, not crosses them
- Someone who listens, not just reacts
- Someone who says "I see you, and I'm not running" without losing themselves in the process

Because trauma shows up as:

- Shutdowns
- Mood swings
- Triggers you didn't cause, but now have to navigate

- Anxiety, depression, detachment, rage, shame

And guess what? You can't love the trauma out of someone.
But you can love them in a way that encourages healing. That means:

- Encouraging therapy, not shaming it
- Being patient, but not self-sacrificing
- Knowing when to step up and when to give space
- Protecting your own peace while supporting theirs

And if you're the one carrying the trauma? Own it. Name it. Don't let it own you. Healing is YOUR job. Not your partner's responsibility.

Here's the law:
Love can't fix trauma, but love can hold hands with healing. The real flex is growing with someone, not in spite of what they've been through.

Healing Together – Yummy's Affirmation Prompt

Repeat this together or alone:

I honor my healing and yours. I release the need to fix, control, or carry what's not mine. I choose patience over pressure, softness over shame, and boundaries over burnout. We are safe, we are growing, and we are not broken. We are becoming.

Law 31: If We Stay, We Gotta Rebuild Real

This Law is critical to me. I personally haven't had to live through this one BUT I have seen it so much around me. I'm talking bout rebuilding after trust is broken. You stayed after the betrayal? Okay then, this ain't for the weak. Law 31 is for the tough hearts who choose to rebuild, not just rebound. Let's talk about what it really means to stay after trust has been shattered, and how to put the pieces back together without losing yourself in the process.

Listen-- trust got broken. A lie. A betrayal. A secret. Maybe even a full-blown "you did WHAT?" situation. Now y'all standing in the aftermath, lookin' around like, "Can this even be saved?"

The answer? Maybe. But not if y'all try to pretend it didn't happen. Not if one of y'all is still lying. Not if the apology is just a performance with no proof.

Rebuilding trust is work, not vibes. It's a contract, not a poem.
It takes:

- Radical honesty, no more sugarcoating
- Real remorse, not just "sorry you found out"
- Changed behavior, not just sweet words
- Recommitment, not just comfort
- Time, and you don't get to rush the timeline

The person who broke the trust gotta humble themselves, consistently show up, and let the other person grieve, question, and process. And the person who was hurt? You have to be real about whether you're healing or holding on just to say you stayed.

Because let's be clear:
Forgiveness is a choice. But reconciliation? That's a mutual rebuild.

And it don't work if you throw it back in their face every argument. Or if they continue to gaslight, you're hurt. You either do the work together or let it go with grace.

Here's the law:
If y'all choose to stay, choose to heal loudly. No fake peace. No performative love. Just real-ass accountability and consistent actions. If we gon' fix this, don't give me gifts, give me change.

Law 32: Endings and New Beginnings

Law 32 is for the ones who know how to let go without losing themselves. This ain't just about heartbreak, it's about release, rebirth, and walking away with your head high and your soul intact. Whether it's the end of a situationship, relationship, or some on-and-off BS that needed to die three summers ago… this chapter is about turning that ending into a beautiful new beginning.

Sometimes love doesn't end with a bang; sometimes it's a slow fade, a quiet ache, or a final straw that breaks in silence. And that's okay.

The end of a relationship isn't always a loss. Sometimes it's a release.
Letting go doesn't mean you didn't love them. It means you loved you enough to move forward.

Let's normalize:

- Breaking up and still wishing them well
- Outgrowing someone without hating them
- Choosing peace over pain, even when it hurts
- Starting over, not as a failure but as a fresh chapter

See, endings reveal what we really need. They teach us:

- What we'll never tolerate again
- What parts of us were left behind
- What kind of love are we now ready to fall in

And new beginnings? Well. That's where you find you again. That's when you remember how to be full without being "claimed." You don't need closure from them, you need clarity within.

Here's the law:
Everything that ends makes space for something better. Mourn it, honor it, but don't stay stuck in it. Because baby… you got bigger love, softer mornings, and realer peace coming.

Law 33: Love Shouldn't Hurt That Long

This is about to get real interesting. I have been waiting to drop this law because I feel real strongly about this. Knowing when to walk away shouldn't become a research paper, thesis, or think piece. We will walk away from everything under the sun but won't walk away from a stupid relationship, a failing relationship, an abusive relationship (whether physically, mentally, or emotionally), just a relationship that's over period. People have to do better with this. You shouldn't feel like you can't walk away from bullshit. Because sometimes the real flex isn't holding on. It's knowing when to dip, with dignity. Let's get into this law for those who stayed too long, prayed too hard, or played therapist when they should have played exit stage left.

Let's get one thing real clear:
You can love someone and still leave.
You can care deeply, hope endlessly, pray daily, and still wake up and say, "This ain't serving me no more."

Knowing when to walk away is spiritual. It's emotional. And yes, it's powerful. Because sometimes staying is what breaks you. And baby, you weren't built to break.

So how do you know it's time?

- When peace feels impossible
- When the apology tour got no new stops
- When your needs always come last
- When you cry more than you laugh
- When you're staying out of fear, guilt, or obligation, not love

Walking away is an act of self-respect, not spite.
You don't owe anyone your forever just because you gave them your yesterday.
Let that sink in.

And let's kill the myth that leaving makes you a quitter. No, baby. It makes you a survivor with boundaries. It makes you someone who chooses their healing over the illusion of love.

You don't have to wait for them to change. You don't gotta wait on one more lie to "finally be the last."
You just gotta choose you. And mean it.

Real talk, a lot of people are stuck in these situationships, marriages, or toxic bonds out of fear, not love. Out of shared bills, not shared peace. Out of raising kids, not building futures. Ok listen I get it… walking away ain't easy (let some of y'all tell it). Especially when the situation comes with kids, money, leases, or shared history that looks good on paper. But let me put it plain:
None of that should trap you in a love that's draining the life out of you. *Shrugs*

Let's talk about the kids.

People stay "for the kids," thinking it's noble. But kids don't need a house full of silence, arguing, resentment, or fake smiles. They need:

- **Two whole, healed parents-** even if those parents live in separate homes
- **A healthy model of love-** not one where Mommy or Daddy is emotionally destroyed
- **Peaceful energy to grow in-** not tension they can feel before they even learn to talk

Kids are not the reason to stay; they should be the reason to leave a toxic situation as soon as possible. Because what you tolerate, they normalize and possibly even grow into thinking those same situations are ok and acceptable. Bullshit. Not fair to them at all.

Now let's talk about finances.

Yes, leaving might mean struggling at first. It might mean tightening up, sleeping on somebody couch, rebuilding credit, working two jobs, or starting over.

But you know what it won't mean?

- Sleeping next to someone who disrespects you
- Losing yourself piece by piece just to keep the lights on
- Dimming your worth so you can split rent

Financial fear is real, but so is financial freedom.
You can rebuild your money. You can't rebuild your soul if it's been broken from staying too long.

And that shared history?

Memories don't make a future. Loyalty is not a life sentence.
If the person you were loyal to ain't loyal to your joy, your growth, or your peace, it's okay to leave.

Here's the truth they don't tell you:
Walking away doesn't mean you failed. It means you woke up.
And waking up is what real love for yourself looks like.

Here's the law:

If staying costs you your self-worth, your joy, your peace, or your glow, it's time to go. With love, with tears, with strength. But go. A real one knows when to leave the table. Especially when all that's being served is crumbs. You can love your kids and still leave. You can be broke and still be brave. You can walk away from what's killing you. Even if it once felt like home.

Law 34: How to Break Up with Compassion

Alright, let's get into it. Because how you leave says a lot about who you really are. Breaking up doesn't always have to be chaotic, cruel, or cold. Sometimes, the most loving thing you can do is leave right.

We all know somebody who dipped out, threw low blows, or disappeared with a new bae like y'all never had history. That's cowardly, not closure. Compassion doesn't mean you stay. It means you leave like somebody who once loved them.

Breaking up with compassion is for people who:

- Don't want bad blood, just better boundaries
- Know love can expire without becoming hate
- Are done with the relationship, but not with humanity

Here's what it looks like:

- **Be direct, not cruel.** Don't drag it out, play mind games, or send mixed signals. Get to the point with care.
- **Speak your truth without blame.** Say what's not working for you, not what's "wrong with them."
- **Give space, not confusion.** After the breakup, don't breadcrumb them or keep calling to "check in." That's not kindness, it's emotional limbo.
- **Acknowledge the good times.** You can honor what it was while still letting it go. Gratitude helps heal.

- **Don't perform the breakup; be present for it.** Look them in the eyes. Feel your feelings. Say what you mean.

And pleaseeeeeee don't stay friends right away just to ease guilt. Let time create space for true peace first. It's okay to disconnect, heal, and maybe reconnect down the line when hearts aren't raw.

Here's the law:
If you loved them at all, don't leave them confused, belittled, or broken. Walk away with clarity, grace, and a lil' grown folk energy. Closure doesn't always come with drama. Sometimes it comes with honesty, hugs, and a final "I wish you the best.".

Law 35: Grieving a Lost Relationship

Now, on the flip side of walking away, there is the aspect of losing that person, and I know that. Which means death isn't the only reason to grieve someone. This law is for the heavy hearts, the silent criers, the overthinkers at 3 a.m., the ones still scrolling through old pics pretending they don't feel that hot, warm feeling in their chest. This one? We gon' sit with it. Because grieving a lost relationship is real, raw, and absolutely necessary. You can't skip this step and expect to be whole. We don't rush healing over here. We ride it out with love and a lil' bit of wisdom.

Let's get it straight:
Breakups don't just end routines, they shatter dreams. They take the future you imagined and put it in the trash with last night's dinner.

Grieving a lost relationship ain't just crying, it's:

- Mourning the "us" that could've been
- Trying to find "you" again in the middle of emotional turmoil
- Unlearning the voice in your head that still sounds like them
- Accepting that sometimes closure doesn't come with answers

You gon' feel it in your chest, in your playlist, in your appetite. You might feel stupid for missing them, mad at yourself for staying so long, or confused about why you still care. And all of that is normal.

This is the detox before the shake back.
This is where your heart stretches so wide, it learns how to hold joy and pain at the same damn time.

Let yourself:

- Cry. Ugly. Loud. Real.
- Write them a letter and never send it.
- Mourn like it's a funeral, 'cause baby… part of your past just died.
- Delete them pics or keep 'em till you're strong enough to look without bleeding.
- Unfollow. Re-follow. Block. Unblock. (No judgment, we've all been there.)

And when it gets heavy?
Remember: you ain't crying over them. You grieving the version of you who thought that love was forever.

And that's deep.

Here's the law:
Grieve like you mean it. Don't numb it, rush it, or shame it. You're not weak, you're HEALING. And that ain't cute, but it's necessary. Grieve loud. Heal slow. Love again. Just don't lose yourself in the process.

Law 36: Reclaiming Your Peace & Power

Looka here, baby, this is the bounce back. The "you thought I was gon' fold, huh?" chapter. The spiritual revenge shake back. After the heartbreak, the crying, the quiet withdrawals, and all the soul-scars, you don't just move on... **You rise up. You reclaim. You reintroduce yourself.** Let's talk about what it really means to take your peace and power back like the healed king/queen you are.

So you've cried, grieved, prayed, and cussed a lil' bit. Now it's time. Time to pick up the pieces and **remind the world who TF you are.** But let's be clear: reclaiming your peace and power isn't about looking good for the 'Gram or making your ex jealous. Nah, this is soul work. This is you saying:

"I'm done bleeding for people who ain't even bandage-worthy."
"I'm not available for chaos anymore."
"I choose me. And I mean that with my whole chest."

Here's how you reclaim that peace & power:

Protect your energy like it's rent due.

If it costs you peace, clarity, or self-worth, it's too expensive. Period. Block numbers, mute triggers, and say no with zero guilt.

Rebuild routines and habits that honor YOU.

Sleep. Hydrate. Take walks. Take mirror pics. Take back your mornings. Make a "no access" list and stick to it. Your nervous system deserves safety.

Ditch the titles. Embrace your truth.

You ain't just someone's ex, someone's old thing, or someone who "used to be…"
You are still powerful. Still divine. Still whole.
That breakup didn't demote your value. It revealed it.

Rewrite your narrative.

You weren't left behind; you were redirected to yourself.
You didn't lose a lover, you lost a lesson that ran its course.

You're not "starting over."
You're starting rooted. With receipts. With purpose.

Let your peace become non-negotiable.

You don't chase closure. You don't explain your boundaries. You don't audition for love.
Your peace is priority. Your power is your presence.

Law 37: From Broken to Brand New

This the rebirth law. Rebuilding yourself after a breakup. The phoenix chapter. The "lemme remind myself who I was before they came and made it messy." You done cried, deleted, healed, journaled in your notes app, blocked, missed them, unblocked, and cried again. And yes fellas you have too. Don't front. Now? It's about the rebuild. The reinvention. The reintroduction.

Let's be all the way real:
A breakup doesn't just end a relationship; it cracks open your sense of identity.
Who you thought you were. Who you were becoming with them.
What y'all were building together. All that crumbles.

So now you're standing there like, "Who TF am I without them?"
This chapter gon' help you answer that, with power, not pain.

Here's How to Rebuild YOU After the Pain:

1. Take Inventory.

Before you rebuild, look at what's still standing. Your strength. Your goals. Your talents. Your joy. Make a list:

- What did I lose in that relationship?
- What did I gain from surviving it?
- What parts of me did I dim to keep the peace?

This is about reclaiming your light. Not their memory.

2. Reclaim Your Routines.

They used to be part of your morning texts, your shows, your weekends? Cool.
Now we reclaim:

- New playlists, new food orders, new hobbies
- Getting fly again just for you
- Creating a home or bedroom that's YOUR vibe
This ain't just moving on, it's moving up.

3. Feed Your Mind & Soul.

Books, therapy, podcasts, prayer, crystals, journaling, gym time.
This is when you go inward and ask:

"Who am I when no one's loving me but me?"

And let that become your favorite version.

4. Romanticize Yourself.

Date you. Compliment you.
Take mirror selfies and thirst trap your own damn camera roll.
Buy flowers for your living room and say, "This is definitely my vibe."

You don't rebuild from shame. You rebuild from self-worship. And no, that ain't cocky, it's healing.

5. Forgive the Version of You Who Didn't Know Better.

Don't shame yourself for what you tolerated, stayed in, or ignored.
Just promise you'll never betray yourself again like that.
That's the rebuild. That's the rebirth. That's the real shakeback.

Law 38: Dating Yourself First

This ain't self-help, it's self-romance. This that "I got me." law. Before you jump into another situationship, lose your mind over good morning texts, or start building a future with somebody who doesn't even know who they are, you need to date the real MVP first. You.

Let's break it down:

A lot of people out here looking for someone to complete them when they ain't even completed their own bio yet. You tryna be boo'd up but don't even know your own love language?
Nah. Before you try to be a lover, be your own damn date.

1. Fall In Love With Your Own Company.

You don't always need a plus one to feel like somebody.

- Go out to eat alone and don't feel weird.
- Go to a movie, take yourself to the spa, sit at the bar in heels with a book.
- Be the type of peace you crave from someone else.
  When you like your own energy, you stop settling for anybody else's.

2. Set the Standard.

Don't wait for someone to treat you right; show them how it's done.

- Buy your own flowers.

- Celebrate your small wins like they matter.
- Talk to yourself sweet.
If you won't even wine and dine you, why would somebody else?

3. Learn Yourself All Over Again.

Date YOU like you tryna make you fall in love.

- Ask yourself deep questions: What do I want now? What turns me on in life? What do I truly deserve?
- Be curious about your growth, your interests, and your evolving dreams.
- Take note of what makes you feel lit up, then do more of that.

4. Be the Energy You Want to Attract.

You want loyalty, peace, ambition, affection? Cool. Give that to you first.
When you become what you desire, you attract people who recognize and respect that frequency. That's how you stop manifesting bums and start calling in kings, queens, and whole healed humans.

Here's the law:

If you can't date you right, don't hand the keys to somebody else who won't.
Self-dating is not just cute. It's crucial.

Law 39: Attracting Healthy Love Only

This that law that's healed, whole, and has high-value energy. We not just looking for love, we attracting what's meant for us. And this time by all means... it better come correct.

You attract what you believe you deserve. So if you still letting dusty energy slide... if you still confusing anxiety for chemistry... if you still thinking "love is hard" means "I gotta suffer for it", this chapter is your detox.

Healthy love ain't loud. It ain't inconsistent. It doesn't have you questioning your worth every minute of the day.

Healthy love is:

- Calm but exciting
- Challenging but respectful
- Safe but not boring
- Honest, warm, and consistent

It sees your scars and kisses them. Not picks at them. It doesn't gaslight you. It guides you. It grows with you. And most importantly? It starts with how you treat yourself.

How to Attract Healthy Love (and Keep It):

1. Heal Your Love Beliefs

If deep down you believe:

- "All relationships are hard."
- "I'm too much"

- "Good love always hurts a little."

…then your nervous system gon' go after that chaos like it's comfort.
Change the love story in your head. Say: "I believe love can be soft, safe, and still pleasing."

2. Detox Your Type

Sometimes your "type" is just your trauma dressed in designer.
Do you keep attracting emotionally unavailable people?
Do you chase validation more than connection?
Baby, rewire your picker. If it doesn't feel peaceful, it ain't healthy.

3. Set Standards, Not Tests

You don't have to "test" people to see if they're worthy.
Just watch them.
Do their words and actions align?
Do they honor your no's?
Do they communicate instead of manipulate?
That's the real test. And healthy love passes it with ease.

4. Be What You Want to Attract

Want honesty? Be honest.
Want consistency? Be consistent.
Want someone healed? Do your healing too.
Don't chase love. Match love.

Law 40: Co-Parenting or Shared Responsibilities Post-Breakup

"It ain't bout you no more. The breakup was between yall. But the responsibility? That still stands." -Yummy

This that "we ain't together no more but we still gotta act right" chapter. This ain't about drama. It's about doing what's right, even when feelings messy. Because real maturity? Shows up even when the love don't live here no more.

You might not mess with your ex like that anymore, and that's valid. But if y'all share kids, bills, a business, or anything that still connects you? You gotta move with structure, not spite. This law right here is about turning your personal pain into a powerful partnership. Even if it's temporary, even if it's from a distance.

This ain't about rekindling anything romantic. It's about creating stability, consistency, and peace for the things and people that still depend on both of y'all to show up.

If Kids Are Involved:

1. Keep the Kids Out the Middle

Your child is not your therapist, messenger, or emotional crutch.
Don't badmouth the other parent to them.
Don't use your child to "get back" at your ex. That's foul and traumatic.

2. Create a Routine That Works

Structure brings peace.
Set schedules, clear pick-up/drop-off plans, split holidays with fairness.
Put it in writing if you have to. **_Consistency over chaos._**

3. Communicate Like Coworkers

Y'all ain't lovers anymore, you're business partners in parenting.
Keep convos short, focused, and respectful.
Use apps, emails, or mediators if necessary.
You ain't gotta like them. Just don't let the kids feel that tension.

If It's Finances or Shared Goals:

- Divide fairly. Be transparent.
- Document everything. Protect your peace.
- Don't let bitterness cost you more than it already has.

Whether it's rent, debt, a shared car note, or a small business...
Handle it like two grown adults who know how to be civil, even if it's hard.

The Real Game-Changer:

This law doesn't mean to be fake.
It means being intentional.
You can grieve the loss and still maintain your integrity.
You can have boundaries and be cooperative.
You can be hurt and still be honorable.

Law 41: Let Them Love You Loudly

"Don't love me in private if you're ashamed of me in public." -Yummy

I feel like Dominic should have written this chapter lol. If they love you, you shouldn't have to beg to be claimed. If they see you as worthy, valuable, and real in their life… It should show. Not just in their texts, but in their tone, their actions, and their presence in your world. This law ain't about being posted on social media. It's about being respected in real life. Because lowkey love feels like a secret. And real love? It stands 10 toes behind you, in front of you, and beside you.

What Loud Love Really Means:

1. They Don't Hide You

You ain't the "just my friend" at functions.
You ain't the "we not putting labels on it" excuse.
You don't gotta wonder who else they're entertaining or why you feel like a placeholder.

Loud love puts a name on it, a claim on it, and makes space for you in all the ways that count.

2. They Protect You in Every Room

Whether you are there or not, your name has value.
They check people who speak sideways to you.
They don't flirt in your absence.
They rep you with pride, not apology.

3. They're Emotionally Present

Loud love doesn't mean loud mouths, it means loud consistency.
They check in. They show up.
They say "I got you" and prove it over and over again.

4. You Never Have to Shrink

You don't feel like you gotta be less "you" to be loved.
They encourage your shine.
They brag on your brilliance.
They match your energy, not mute it.

But If You Gotta Wonder…

- Why they never post you?
- Why they act different around certain people?
- Why their phone always flipped down?
- Why you feel like a "good time" but not a real thing?

…Then maybe you not being loved out loud. Maybe you just being kept quiet for their convenience. And that ain't love. That's a liability.

Law 42: When Love Feels Safe

Let's be real, a lot of us were raised on chaos, drama, negative shit, etc. Toxic love felt like home. Passion meant pain. You thought love was supposed to hurt a little, didn't you? That it had to be full of ups, downs, breakups, and makeup to be "real"?

Nah man. That wasn't love. That was survival mode.

Safe Love Hits Different:

1. Your Mind Feels Clear

No guessing games.
No decoding texts or tone.
You're not constantly replaying convos or wondering what you did wrong.

You just... relax.
Your thoughts ain't racing. Your heart ain't breaking every weekend.

2. You Can Breathe Around Them

You're not performing.
You're not shrinking.
You don't have to wear a mask to be loved.
They see you with your flaws and all and still hold you with tenderness.

3. You Feel Heard and Held

They don't dismiss your feelings.
They don't punish you for being vulnerable.

Safe love leans in when things get hard.
You don't have to beg to be understood.

4. They Show Up, Over and Over

Safe love is consistent.
It honors your boundaries, respects your pace, and celebrates your growth.
No threats. No walking on eggshells. Just mutual protection, effort, and trust.

What Safe Love *Ain't*

- It's not boring.
- It's not emotionless.
- It's not "settling."
  It's peace. And peace is passion that doesn't burn you.

Here's the law:

Love isn't supposed to be a warzone. If I gotta fight for peace, it ain't love, it's trauma.

Law 43: Knowing When You're Ready Again

"I'm not rushing to be chosen. I've already chosen me." -Yummy

Everybody wanna love and be loved. But let's keep it a stack, jumping into something too fast? That's how you end up repeating patterns. Same pain, different person. Same lessons, new heartbreak. Knowing when you're genuinely ready again means you've done the inner groundwork. Not just moved on physically, but moved forward emotionally, mentally, and spiritually.

Ask Yourself These 5 Real Ones:

1. Do I Still Speak on My Ex... A Lot?

If their name stays in rotation, good or bad, you still connected.
Healing means detachment. Not avoidance, not bitterness. Just peace with the past.

2. Am I Looking for a Healer or a Partner?

If you're hoping someone "fixes" your pain, you ain't ready.
You need a partner, not a prescription.

3. Can I Handle Disappointment Without Breaking?

When you're healed, you can date without spiraling.
You don't put your worth in someone else's response.

You know how to bounce back without losing yourself.

4. Do I Know What I Actually Want Now?

Not just what you don't want…
Knowing what you do want. In a partner. In a connection. In life.

5. Can I Be Happy Alone First?

This the big one.
Because if your joy only shows up when someone's around?
You ain't ready to share a table, you still building your plate.

Signs You Might Be Ready:

- You're not bitter. You're just better.
- You date with discernment, not desperation.
- You trust yourself again.
- You're not afraid of love, you just don't chase it.
- You feel whole, not half, not hunted.

Law 44: The Art of Intentional Dating

"Date with a purpose or don't date at all." - Yummy

Intentional dating doesn't mean you're trying to marry everybody you text. It means you're moving with clarity, confidence, and standards, not confusion. This law is about dating in a way that's aligned with your values, not your voids. Because if you date out of boredom, fear, or ego… You gonna keep ending up with people who feel fun but are not fulfilling. Nice pic, but chaotic in real life.

Intentional Dating Means:

1. You Know Your Why

Are you dating to build? To explore? To heal? Knowing your why helps you filter out who's aligned and who's wasting time.

2. You Communicate What You Want

Early and often.
Not "go with the flow," not "let's just see what happens."
You let folks know, this is where I'm headed. Are we on the same road or nah?

3. You're Real With Yourself

You don't date people you think you can fix.
You don't entertain folks just 'cause you're lonely.
You peep the red flags and don't paint 'em green.

4. You Set Boundaries Without Apology

Your time, energy, and body are not on clearance. You don't owe anybody unlimited access just because they're cute or consistent.
Intentional dating honors your peace over pressure.

What It's *Not*:

- It's not rushing.
- It's not being overly picky.
- It's not being cold-hearted or "too serious." It's just saying: "I know what I bring, and I'm not settling for vibes when I deserve vision."

Law 45: Stop Ignoring Your Intuition (The Gut Never Lies)

Let's keep it funky, your body knows before your brain catches up. The shift in their tone. The late replies. The tension you can't name. That off feeling when they said "they just need space." You felt it. You knew it. You just didn't listen.

What Is Intuition?

It's your internal alarm system.
It's not loud or dramatic. It's subtle, soft, sacred.
A voice that whispers:

"Something don't sit right."
"They lying."
"You deserve more."
"Let go."

And too many times, we ignore it because we want fairy tales more than we want the truth.

How Ignoring Your Gut Shows Up:

- Overriding red flags with excuses.
- Holding onto potential instead of patterns.
- Letting "chemistry" cancel out common sense.
- Staying just to avoid starting over.
- Convincing yourself it's "just your trauma," when really it's your wisdom trying to speak.

The Truth?

Your intuition ain't out to hurt you, it's out to protect you.
It don't care about your timeline, your type, or your situationship status.
It cares about your peace, your purpose, and your power.

Law 46: Polyamory, Open Relationships, and Ethical Non-Monogamy

"Poly Me." -Yummy

Now that you have been through all that, this law dives briefly into the different types of relationships you might be looking at after all the foolishness you went through. Because you may have realized after giving your all to someone and it failed, that type of relationship isn't for you anymore. This is where we throw out shame, unpack labels, and step into truth. This ain't about what's "normal", this is about what's honest, consensual, and aligned.

Let's set the record straight, polyamory ain't about sex. It's about structure, honesty, and capacity. It ain't a trend. It ain't an excuse to cheat. And it damn sure ain't "easier" than monogamy.

What It Really Is:

- **Polyamory** = Having multiple loving relationships with everyone's full knowledge and consent.
- **Open Relationships** = You may have a primary partner but can connect intimately or sexually with others.
- **Ethical Non-Monogamy (ENM)** = Any relationship setup that isn't exclusive but stays rooted in honesty, communication, and consent.

Before You Try It, Ask Yourself:

1. Am I Emotionally Mature Enough for This?

This lifestyle takes radical communication, trust, and personal accountability.
It's not for the jealous, petty, or passive-aggressive.

2. Am I Doing This to Heal... or to Hide?

You can't use poly to cover up your fear of commitment, your cheating past, or your fear of being alone.
If you can't do monogamy with integrity, you damn sure can't do poly with it.

3. Do I Actually Understand It Or Just Want Options?

Don't play with people's hearts just 'cause you want a hall pass.
ENM works when it's done ethically, not secretly.

Common Myths (Let's Bust 'Em):

Myth: "Poly people don't believe in commitment."
Truth: Nah, they just don't believe one person has to meet every single need.

Myth: "It's just about sex."
Truth: Most poly folks want connection, not just bodies.

Myth: "Jealousy doesn't exist in poly."
Truth: Jealousy shows up, it just gets talked about, not weaponized.

Tips for Doing It Ethically:

- Set clear agreements with each person.
- Check in constantly, feelings change, so should boundaries.
- Never compare your partners to each other.
- Learn the difference between freedom and recklessness.

Law 47: Keeping It Real About What You Want

Let's be for real, most people don't get what they want in relationships because they never say what they want. They drop hints. They hope. They wait for the other person to read their mind. And when that don't work, they settle. But baby, I'm not in the business of pretending to be low maintenance just to be liked. Speak up or stay unsatisfied. This that law many of us skip over.

What This Law Is About:

- Being honest with yourself first, about your needs, desires, and boundaries.
- Then being honest with others, no sugarcoating, no shrinking, no silent suffering.

Whether it's love, consistency, space, sex, exclusivity, communication, attention, affection, freedom, or structure, you gotta ask for it, expect it, and walk away if it ain't being respected.

Signs You're Not Keeping It Real:

- You downplay what you really want to "keep the peace."
- You let red flags slide because you're scared they'll leave.
- You convince yourself to be "chill" when you really want something solid.
- You wait for them to "figure it out" instead of just telling them.

Real Love Requires Real Talk:
You want to be wife'd up? Say that.
You want space to grow individually? Say that.

You want monogamy? Say that.
You want your back blown out three times a week and flowers every week? Shit say that too.

Because the right one for you will never be scared off by your truth.
And if they are? **That's not your person.**

Law 48: Gender Roles and Evolving Dynamics

The final law? Oh let me close this thing with a grown-ass conversation then. This that "we not doing it like grandma and papa if it don't serve us" law. This that "gender roles been weak asf, let's evolve" law. This not about feminine or masculine but just be a human in the situation. How about that.

Back in the day, it was "so simple" (and simple-minded). The men brought home the bacon. The ladies cooked the bacon, raised the babies, and never complained. But we ain't back in the day. We in an era where roles are chosen, not assigned. Where a man can cook, cry, and lead with softness. Where a woman can boss up, protect her peace, and still be soft when she feel safe.

Real Talk:

Gender roles used to keep the house in order. Now they just keep people out of alignment. Because when you're playing a role, you might end up playing yourself.

What Evolved Love Looks Like:

- **We build based on strengths, not stereotypes.**
  She might be better at money. He might be better at parenting. That don't make nobody less of anything.
- **Both people contribute, in whatever way works.**
  This ain't "you pay bills, I cook." This is, "we co-create a life that makes sense for us."

- **Soft men aren't weak. Powerful women aren't cold.**
  Masculinity and femininity don't come with rules. They come with energy, balance, and emotional fluency.
- **We don't shame, we shift.**
  If he wants to stay home and raise the kids? Cool.
  If she wanna be the breadwinner? Cool.
  The only thing that's "wrong" is pretending to be something you're not.

Let's Reframe:

Old Way	New Way
"Men don't show emotion"	"Men process and express their feelings"
"Women belong in the home"	"Women belong wherever they choose"
"A real man pays for everything"	"A real man contributes with pride, not ego"
"Submission means silence"	"Submission means mutual trust and flow"

Here's the law:

Let go of the idea that being a "real man" or a "real woman" is about roles. It's about character, communication, and commitment. Your gender doesn't define your value. Your energy does. If you need help, ask. If you're tired, say so. If the dynamic no longer serves you, change it, together. Because love that's built on who does what will crumble under pressure. But love that's built on mutual respect, teamwork, and emotional equity? That's unshakeable. We are not doing relationships to impress tradition. We are doing it to express truth. Love evolves when people do.

Yummy

Yummy's Type of Love is a Lifestyle, Not a Phase

This ain't just a book. It's a whole blueprint for real love, real growth, and real freedom. Whether you're monogamous, poly, healing, or whole, you deserve love that's aligned, not assigned. You made it through all 48 laws. That means you didn't just read this book, you walked with it, sat in it, felt it. You didn't just want relationships, you wanted real ones.

It's not just for the "right time" or the "right person." It's not something you grow out of or age into. These laws are a mindset. A rhythm. A vibration you live by. It doesn't matter if you are 17, 27, 47, or 67, this love applies to ALL stages.

And with those stages, it's levels to how love usually plays out. Consider this: in your teens, you are learning the distinction between attention and intention. In your 20s, you learn raw lessons, go through heartbreaks, and figure out who tf you are. When you hit your midlife, that's when you want substance, peace, and partnership with depth. And lastly towards your later life, that's when you love freely, finally, and without apology, because you've earned it.

Love meets you wherever you are. No shame. No pressure. No clock. Just truth.

This book was never just about relationships. It was about you. The version of you that knows better now. The version of you that refuses to shrink, settle, or suffer in silence.

Remember, don't chase love, align with it. Don't shrink your love, expand it even more. Don't beg for love, become the love YOU desire.

This ain't the end, Love. This is just your beginning.

Reflection and Rejection: The Yummy that Never got Picked

I gotta be real with yall before I close this book. I've written about love, relationships, healing, and power, but the truth is… I've never even been in a relationship. Not because I didn't try. Not because I wasn't ready. But because every woman I tried to want or love rejected me for one thing: I'm a big guy.

I wasn't lazy. I wasn't mean. I wasn't toxic. I wasn't broken. I was just big. And for some reason, in their eyes, that was enough. They never even took the time to get to know me. Every time I tried to shoot my shot, I got met with looks, laughs, or fake kindness that still cut like shade. They said I was "cool, but not their type." Or "Yummy is sweet". They wanted the personality, but not the presence. They wanted the vibe, but not the weight.

And the women who did give me attention came with some silly ass rules. Weird double standards. They'd want me to act taken while they still engaged in baby daddy activities. They'd want me to change how I lived, how I existed, but they weren't offering that same energy back. I've been through it all when it comes to rejection. I have had ladies lead me like they like me but nah, get married on me, play in my face, holla at my potnas, you name it.

That kind of rejection doesn't just hurt. It shapes you. It makes you question your worth. It makes you wonder, "Am I only lovable if I'm smaller?", "Do I gotta shrink myself physically or emotionally to be wanted?". But over time, I realized the answer was no. I don't have to become what makes them comfortable. They just weren't ready for this kind of love. They weren't ready for a man who loves deeply, thinks differently, and doesn't fit the fake mold. And that's okay because I'm super good now. And before I started thinking and feeling this way, I was literally ready to settle for anything and with whoever would have me. Just to say I'm with somebody. I'm glad I didn't, though. I was gone be miserable as hell. I'm free. No drama, no baggage, no nothing when it comes to that. So, when my time comes, the special lady will win.

 See, this book? This whole "Yummy Type of Love" concept? It came from being on the outside of love and still choosing to believe in it. Still choosing to define it for myself. I may have never been chosen, but I'm still the prize.

Why I Wrote This Book: Inspired by Power, Game & Real Love

I got to keep it real, this book wouldn't exist without *The 48 Laws of Power, The 50th Law,* and *Pimpology: The 48 Laws of the Game.* Not because I wanted to copy them, but because I loved how they broke down real strategy, survival, self-respect, and raw truth, especially in systems designed to play us.

I read *The 48 Laws of Power* and saw how people protect themselves in a cold world. I read *The 50th Law* and felt the fearlessness it takes to stand on your story. I read *Pimpology: The 48 Laws of the Game* and saw a whole code of conduct. One that, while street, still highlighted structure, psychology, and influence.

But what didn't I see?

A guide on how to fall in love with that same discipline. How to hold your standards in relationships like you do in the streets, in the boardroom, or at the mic. How to be smooth but solid. Vulnerable but not weak. Loving but not lost.

So, I flipped the game.

I took the blueprint and gave it the Yummy perspective. Made it about intimacy, trust, emotional intelligence, and respect. Because love is power too. And if we gon' play the game, we need rules that actually protect our hearts, not just our pride.

The 48 Laws of Yummy Are Different

This ain't about manipulation. It's about maturity. This ain't about domination. It's about discernment. This ain't about control. It's about clarity. These laws don't just help you win love, they help you win with yourself. Because once you learn how to love on your own terms, once you set boundaries that feel holy, once you walk away from confusion with your head high and your heart unbothered. You don't chase peace, you become it.

Final Word

I wrote this book because power without love is hollow. And love without game is reckless.

But love, with Yummy Laws? That's unshakable. That's yours. And you can't lose.

Acknowledgments

To my Pops, Ron P., me and you against the world Pops. I told you I got us and I meant it. I'ma carry this Pujoe name with grace and create a legacy that will be forever in thy name. We P.

To my family, thank you for being my foundation. Every lesson, every moment, every ounce of love (even the tough kind) shaped the way I see the world and helped me become who I am. Your presence, your prayers, and your protection have meant everything.

To my home girls and potnas, thank you for riding with me through the bad, the magic, the late-night rants, and the real-life therapy sessions we called conversation. Your encouragement, honesty, laughter, and light kept me going when the realities of this book felt heavy. Some of y'all helped me heal from rejection and such just by listening. Some of y'all were the blueprint for the laws themselves. Either way, I see you, and I love you.

To those who doubted me or dismissed me because I didn't fit the image, thank you too. You gave me the motivation. You gave me the purpose. And now I'm using both.

This book is for anyone who's ever felt unseen, misunderstood, or unloved. It's for those who've been rejected, overlooked, or underestimated and still chose to love anyway. This is our love language. Our laws. Our legacy.

With all my heart,

LeShaun D. Pujoe

References

Chapman, G. (2010). The 5 love languages: The secret to love that lasts. Chicago, IL: Northfield Publishing.

www.ingramcontent.com/pod-product-compliance
Lightning Source LLC
Chambersburg PA
CBHW031634160426
43196CB00006B/418